Ensemble Music
for
Group Piano

Fourth Edition

by

James Lyke
Professor of Music, Emeritus
University of Illinois, Urbana-Champaign

Geoffrey Haydon
Associate Professor of Music
Georgia State University, Atlanta

Pubished by
STIPES PUBLISHING COMPANY
204 West University Avenue
Champaign, Illinois 61820

To Denise Edwards

Design, Layout, and Cover Image by
CP Music Engraving, Chicago, Illinois

ISBN 1-58874-136-2

P R E F A C E

to the Fourth Edition

The 4th edition of Ensemble Music For Group Piano is designed to provide supplementary piano ensemble music for college and university piano classes and multi-keyboard private studios. Written for students beyond the beginning level, the book may be used in the second, third and fourth semesters of college study or for several years in private studios to develop ensemble, musicianship and performing skills.

Ensemble Music For Group Piano (EMGP) is divided into three sections. Section One contains music for one piano-four hands (1P4H). With easy primo parts written in major and minor five-finger patterns, these works include a variety of keys and rhythms and lend themselves to sight-reading, rapid learning and the myriad challenges of ensemble playing. The difficulty level in Section One ranges from elementary to lower intermediate. Many duets are suitable for performance in recital programs, and, in college piano classes, some may be used to measure progress.

Section Two consists of 1P4H pieces beyond the five-finger range. Many of these works are original (Beethoven, Tchaikovsky, Persichetti, etc.) and others are arranged. In this section students should play both primo and secondo parts. Because many students studying piano at the secondary level are instrumentalists who have experience in only one clef, this section provides necessary training in an unfamiliar clef. (For example, a violinist would benefit from intensive bass clef training that secondo parts provide.) The playing level of Section Two ranges roughly from lower-intermediate to intermediate. Section Two is arranged chronologically by musical era—from Ludwig van Beethoven to Irving Berlin. The thoughtful teacher will select duets to develop musicianship and technical skills as well as an understanding of various styles. In addition, many secondo parts lend themselves to rapid harmonic analysis and may be used for special study and transposition.

Section Three features music for two, three, five and six pianos. The two-piano section is arranged by era, from J.S. Bach (Minuet in G) to American song composer Vincent Youmans (Bambalina). Music for multiple pianos (beyond two) may be used for sight-reading as well as piano festival concerts. Students will want to explore various sampled sounds on their digital keyboards (strings, flutes, percussion, etc.) to enhance the excerpts from Beethoven and Schubert symphonies.

The 4th edition of EMGP includes a play-a-long CD (or 3.5 inch SMF disk available from the publisher at no extra charge). The tracks have been digitally recorded by co-author Dr. Geoffrey Haydon of Georgia State University, Atlanta. Sections One, Two and the first part of Section Three are completely recorded. Music for three, five and six pianos is not recorded.

Ensemble Music for Group Piano

TABLE OF CONTENTS

Section One
Works for One Piano-Four Hands with
5-Finger Position Primo Parts in Major and Minor

MAJOR 5-FINGER PRIMO PATTERNS

Melodious Piece, Op. 149, No. 3 . . . . .Diabelli 2–5
Melodious Piece, Op. 149, No. 4 . . . . .Diabelli 6–7
Evening . . . . .Löw 8–9
Moderato Cantabile (from *First Steps*) . . . .Maykapar 10–13
Melodious Piece, Op. 149, No. 8 . . . . .Diabelli 14–15
Andante Cantabile, Op. 6, No. 3 . . . . .Enke 16–17
Melodious Piece, Op. 149, No. 9 . . . . .Diabelli 18–19
On Horseback, Op. 74, No. 2 . . . . .Cui 20–21
Hunting, Op. 81, No. 3 . . . . .Gurlitt 22–23

MINOR 5-FINGER PRIMO PATTERNS

Funeral For A Bird, Op. 74, No. 1 . . . . . . .Cui 24–25
Allegretto in C Minor . . . . .Gurlitt 26–27
Mama Scolds, Op. 74, No. 4 . . . . .Cui 28–29
Romance in A Minor, Op. 6, No. 1 . . . . . . .Enke 30–31
Romance in G Minor. Op. 149, No. 11 . . . .Diabelli 32–33
Gray Day, Op. 74, No. 3 . . . . .Cui 34–35

Section Two
Original Works and Arrangements for One Piano-Four Hands

German Dance in C . . . . .Beethoven 36–37
German Dance in B♭ . . . . .Beethoven 38–39
Dance, Op. 824, No. 18 . . . . .Czerny 40–41
Allegro Non Troppo . . . . .Maykapar 42–45
Lændler . . . . .Schubert 46–47
My Braids . . . . .Tchaikovsky 48–49
There Was No Wind . . . . .Tchaikovsky 48–49
Vanya . . . . .Tchaikovsky 50–51
At The Gate . . . . .Tchaikovsky 50–51
Little Piece in G . . . . .Bruckner 52–53
I Saw Three Ships . . . . .arr. Ferguson 54–57

Ensemble Music for Group Piano

Round Dance . . . . .Bartok, *arr.* Suchoff .58–59

Balalaika (from *Five Easy Pieces*) . . . . . . .Stravinsky 60–63

Serenade No. 8, Op. 62 . . . . .Persichetti 64–65

Playtime . . . . .Dello Joio 66–69

Alexander's Ragtime Band . . . . .Berlin, *arr.* Haydon *and* Lyke 70–73

Wonderful One . . . . .Whiteman *and* Grofe, *arr.* Haydon *and* Lyke 74–77

Limehouse Blues . . . . .Braham, *arr.* Haydon *and* Lyke 78–81

Section Three
Arrangements for Multiple Pianos or Keyboards

TWO PIANOS OR KEYBOARDS

Sarabanda . . . . .Corelli, *arr.* Last 82–84

Minuet in G . . . . .Bach, *arr.* Lee 85–87

Minuet . . . . .Haydn, *arr.* Anson 88–89

Andante in E♭ . . . . .Mozart, *arr.* Haydon *and* Lyke 90

Waltz in B Minor . . . . .Schubert, *arr.* Haydon *and* Lyke 91–93

Canon . . . . .Schumann, *arr.* Haydon *and* Lyke 94

Bambalina . . . . .Youmans, *arr.* Haydon *and* Lyke 95–97

Dawn . . . . .Caramia 98–99

THREE PIANOS OR KEYBOARDS

Slow Movement Theme from

Symphony No. 7 . . . . .Beethoven, *arr.* Smith 100–101

FIVE PIANOS OR KEYBOARDS

Main Theme, Third Movement from

Symphony No. 3 . . . . .Brahms, *arr.* Smith .102–103

SIX PIANOS OR KEYBOARDS

Lullaby . . . . .Brahms, *arr.* Keck .104–105

Jeanie With The Light Brown Hair . . . . . . .Foster, *arr.* Keck .106–108

The Band Played On . . . . .Ward, *arr.* Keck 109–113

Trio from Symphony No. 7 . . . . .Schubert, *arr.* Smith 114–119

CD/MIDI Tracks 120

Table of Contents

Section One: Major and Minor 5-Finger Primo Patterns

SECTION ONE
Major 5-Finger Primo Patterns (1P4H)

MELODIOUS PIECE
(Op. 149, No. 3)

SECONDO

Anton Diabelli

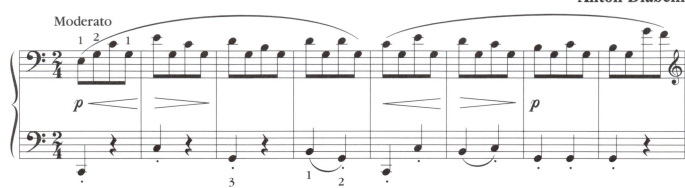

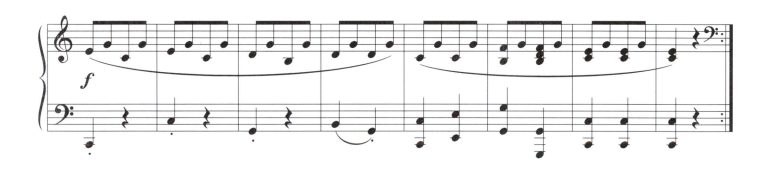

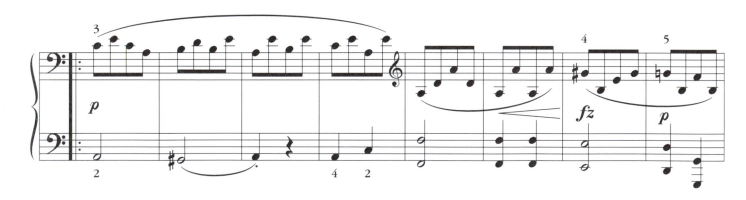

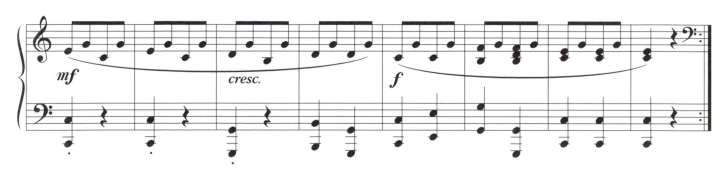

Ensemble Music for Group Piano

MELODIOUS PIECE

(Op. 149, No. 3)

PRIMO

Anton Diabelli

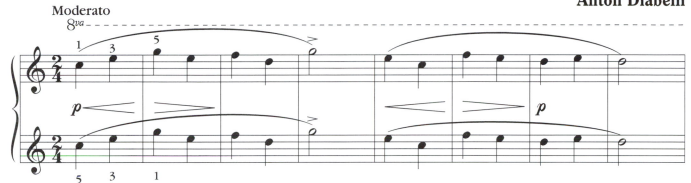

Section One: Major 5-Finger Primo Patterns

SECONDO

PRIMO

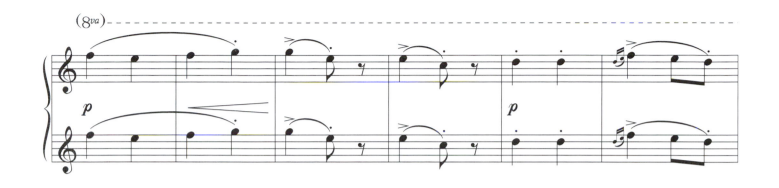

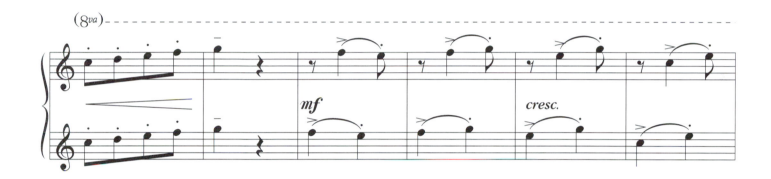

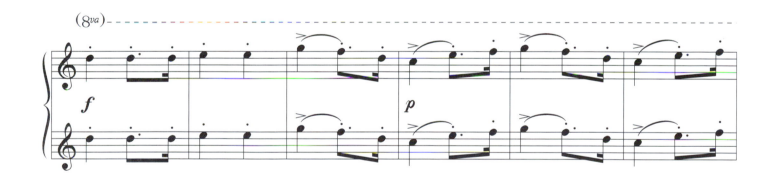

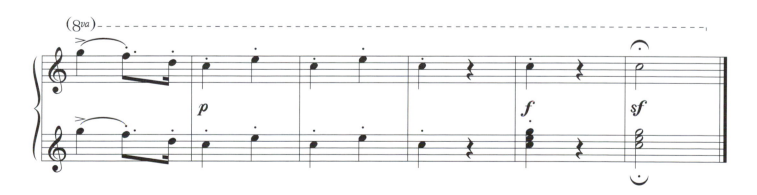

Section One: Major 5-Finger Primo Patterns

MELODIOUS PIECE
(Op. 149, No. 4)
SECONDO

Anton Diabelli

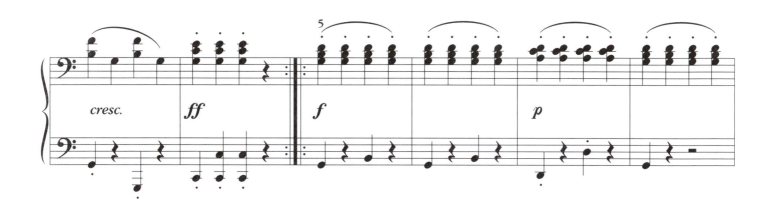

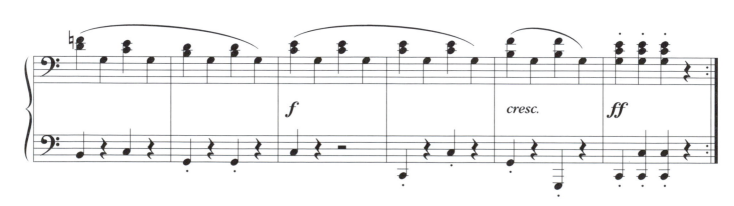

Ensemble Music for Group Piano

MELODIOUS PIECE
(Op. 149, No. 4)

PRIMO

Anton Diabelli

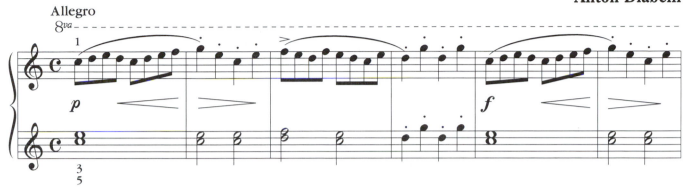

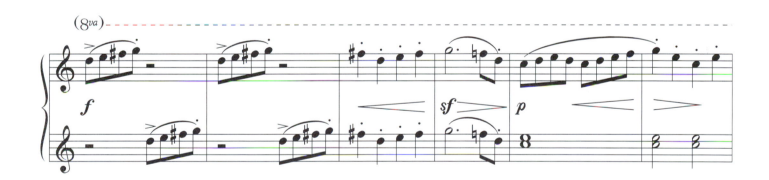

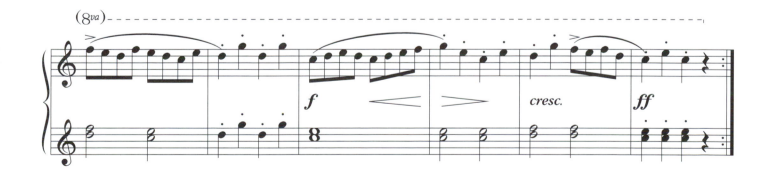

Section One: Major 5-Finger Primo Patterns

EVENING
SECONDO

Josef Löw

EVENING

PRIMO

Josef Löw

Section One: Major 5-Finger Primo Patterns

MODERATO CANTABILE
(from *First Steps*)
SECONDO

Samuel Maykapar

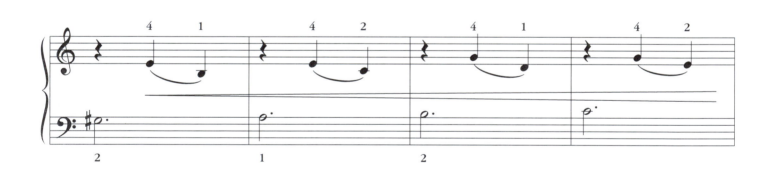

MODERATO CANTABILE *

(from *First Steps*)

PRIMO

Samuel Maykapar

* *Moderato Cantabile's* primo part is written in a B diminished pattern. The key, however, is C major.

Section One: Major 5-Finger Primo Patterns

SECONDO

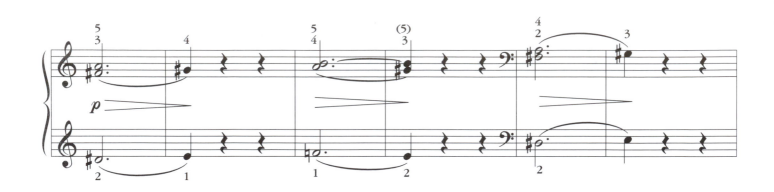

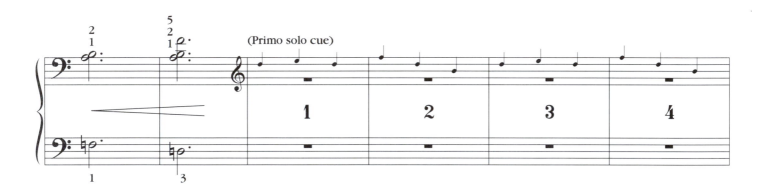

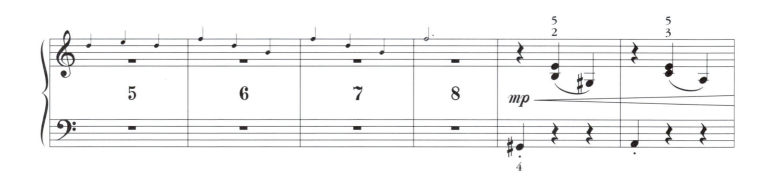

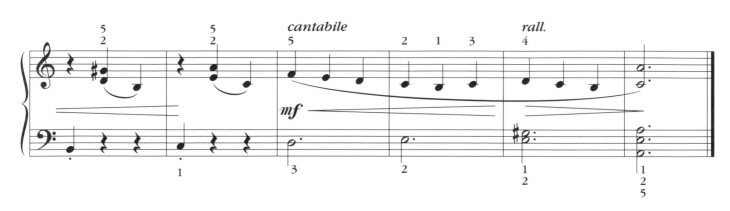

Ensemble Music for Group Piano

PRIMO

Section One: Major 5-Finger Primo Patterns

MELODIOUS PIECE

(Op. 149, No. 8)

SECONDO

Anton Diabelli

Ensemble Music for Group Piano

MELODIOUS PIECE
(Op. 149, No. 8)

PRIMO

Anton Diabelli

Section One: Major 5-Finger Primo Patterns

ANDANTE CANTABILE
(Op. 6, No. 3)
SECONDO

Heinrich Enke

ANDANTE CANTABILE

(Op. 6, No. 3)

PRIMO

Heinrich Enke

Section One: Major 5-Finger Primo Patterns

MELODIOUS PIECE

(Op. 149, No. 9)

SECONDO

Anton Diabelli

MELODIOUS PIECE
(Op. 149, No. 9)
PRIMO

Anton Diabelli

Section One: Major 5-Finger Primo Patterns

ON HORSEBACK
(Op. 74, No. 2)
SECONDO

César Cui

ON HORSEBACK
(Op. 74, No. 2)
PRIMO

César Cui

Section One: Major 5-Finger Primo Patterns

HUNTING
(Op. 81, No. 3)
SECONDO

Cornelius Gurlitt

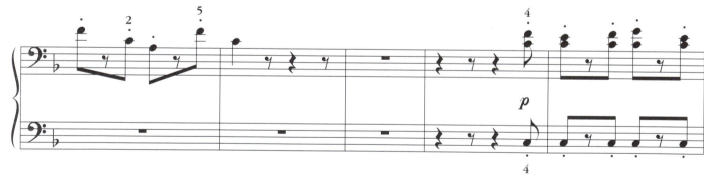

HUNTING
(Op. 81, No. 3)
PRIMO

Cornelius Gurlitt

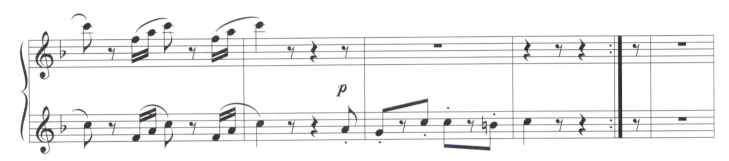

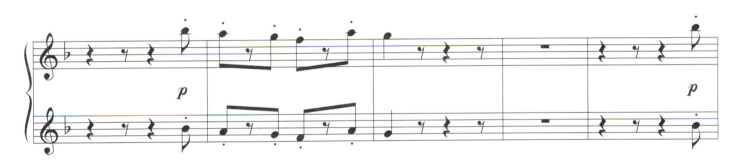

Section One: Major 5-Finger Primo Patterns

SECTION ONE
Minor 5-Finger Primo Patterns (1P4H)

10

FUNERAL FOR A BIRD
(Op, 74, No. 1)

SECONDO

César Cui

FUNERAL FOR A BIRD

(Op. 74, No. 1)

PRIMO

César Cui

Section One: Minor 5-Finger Primo Patterns

ALLEGRETTO IN C MINOR

SECONDO

Cornelius Gurlitt

Allegretto Scherzando

ALLEGRETTO IN C MINOR

PRIMO

Cornelius Gurlitt

Section One: Minor 5-Finger Primo Patterns

MAMA SCOLDS
(Op. 74, No. 4)
SECONDO

César Cui

Moderato

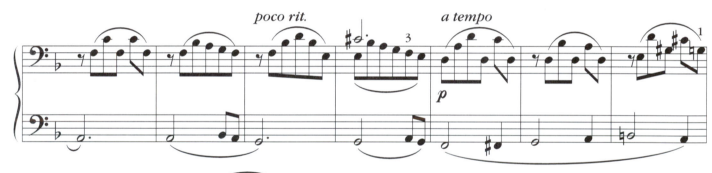

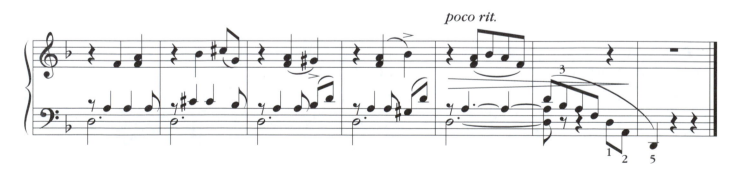

MAMA SCOLDS

(Op. 74, No. 4)

PRIMO

César Cui

Section One: Minor 5-Finger Primo Patterns

ROMANCE IN A MINOR

(Op. 6, No. 1)

SECONDO

Heinrich Enke

ROMANCE IN A MINOR

(Op. 6, No. 1)

PRIMO

Heinrich Enke

Section One: Minor 5-Finger Primo Patterns

ROMANCE IN G MINOR
(Op. 149, No. 11)

SECONDO

Anton Diabelli

Moderately flowing

ROMANCE IN G MINOR

(Op. 149, No. 11)

PRIMO

Anton Diabelli

Section One: Minor 5-Finger Primo Patterns

GRAY DAY
(Op. 74, No. 3)

SECONDO

César Cui

GRAY DAY

(Op. 74, No. 3)

PRIMO

César Cui

Section One: Minor 5-Finger Primo Patterns

SECTION TWO
Original Works and Arrangements (1P4H)

GERMAN DANCE IN C
SECONDO

Ludwig van Beethoven

GERMAN DANCE IN C

PRIMO

Ludwig van Beethoven

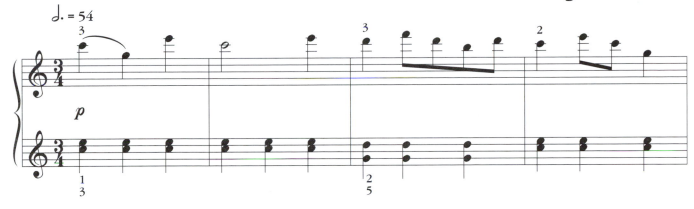

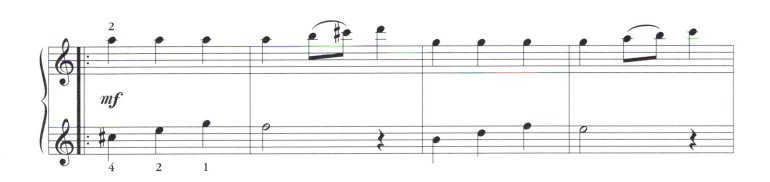

Section Two: Original Works and Arrangements

18 GERMAN DANCE IN B♭

SECONDO

Ludwig van Beethoven

Ensemble Music for Group Piano

GERMAN DANCE IN B♭

PRIMO

Ludwig van Beethoven

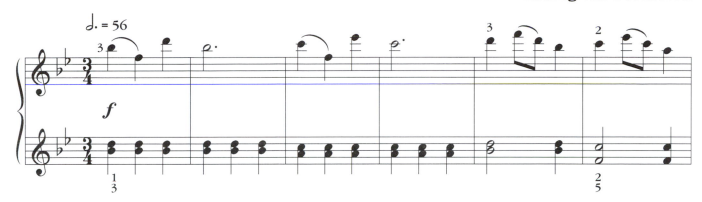

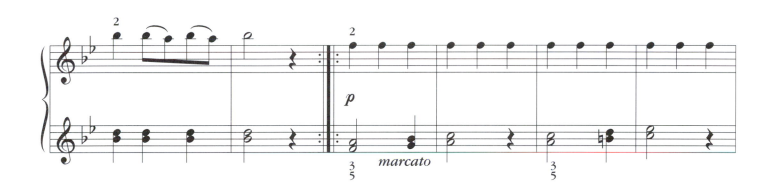

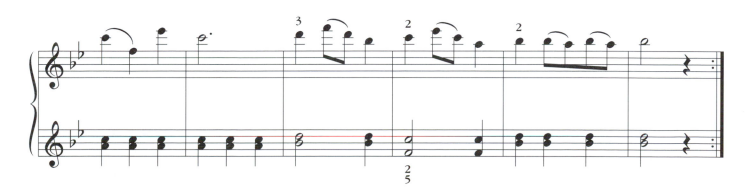

Section Two: Original Works and Arrangements

DANCE
(Op. 824 , No.18)

SECONDO

Carl Czerny

Allegretto

Ensemble Music for Group Piano

DANCE
(Op. 824, No. 18)
PRIMO

Carl Czerny

Section Two: Original Works and Arrangements

ALLEGRO NON TROPPO

SECONDO

Samuel Maykapar

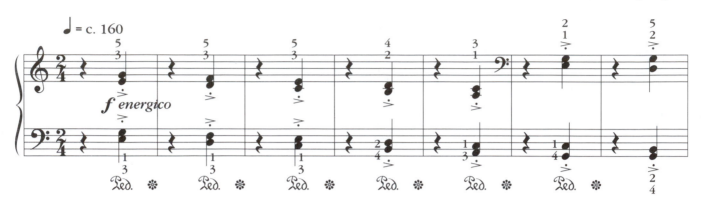

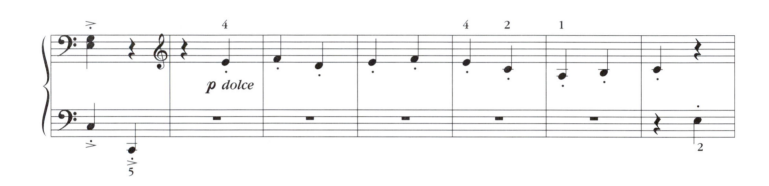

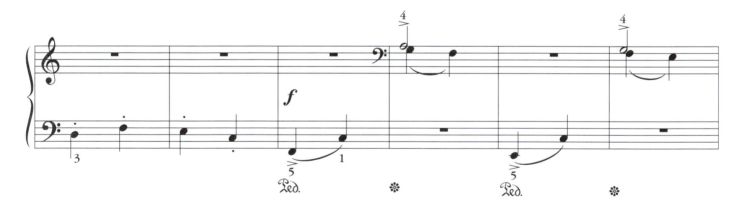

Ensemble Music for Group Piano

ALLEGRO NON TROPPO

PRIMO

Samuel Maykapar

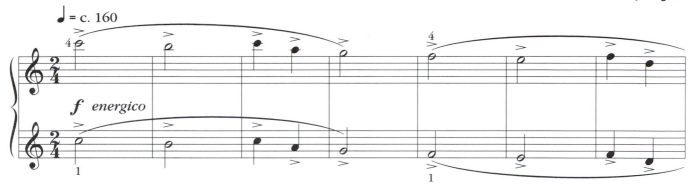

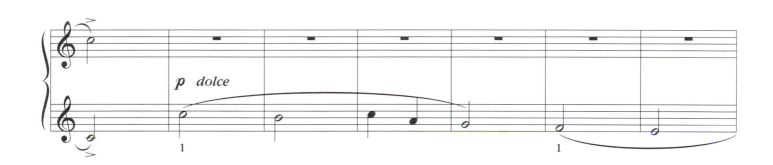

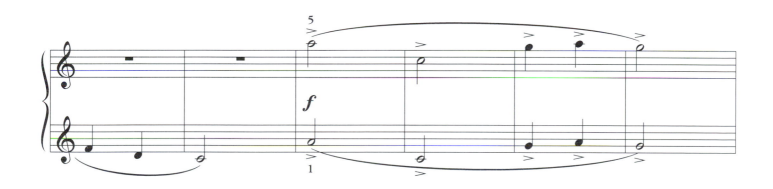

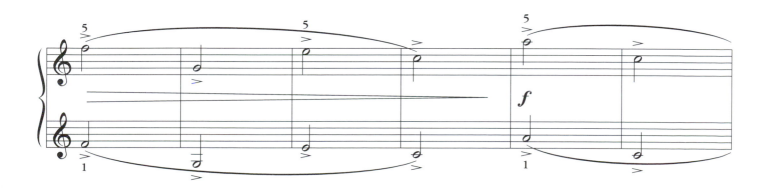

Section Two: Original Works and Arrangements

SECONDO

PRIMO

Section Two: Original Works and Arrangements

LÆNDLER
SECONDO

Franz Schubert

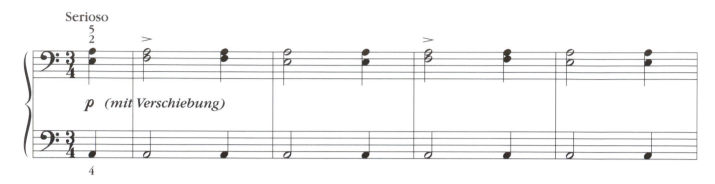

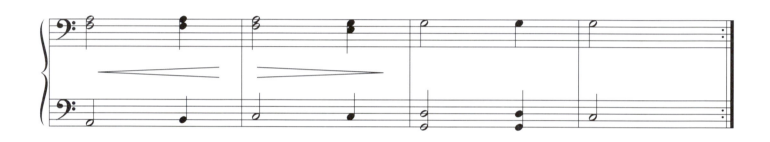

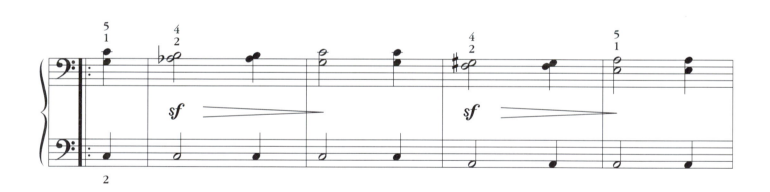

Ensemble Music for Group Piano

LÆNDLER

PRIMO

Franz Schubert

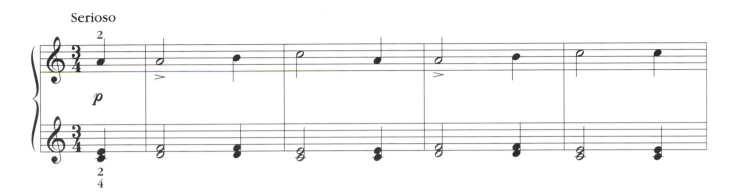

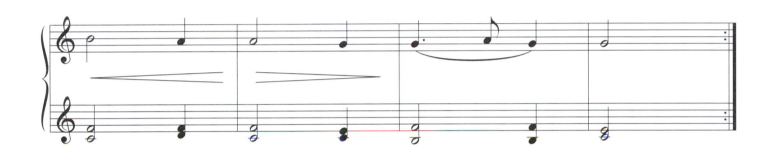

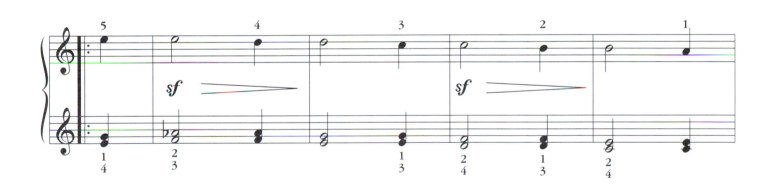

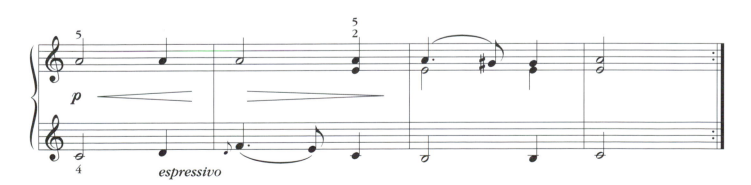

Section Two: Original Works and Arrangements

MY BRAIDS
SECONDO

Peter I. Tchaikovsky

THERE WAS NO WIND
SECONDO

Peter I. Tchaikovsky

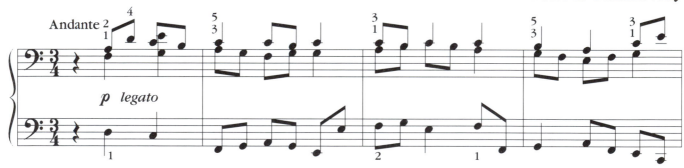

Ensemble Music for Group Piano

MY BRAIDS
PRIMO

Peter I. Tchaikovsky

THERE WAS NO WIND
PRIMO

Peter I. Tchaikovsky

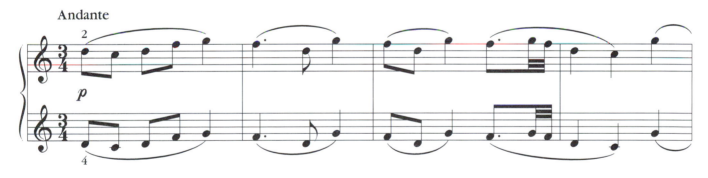

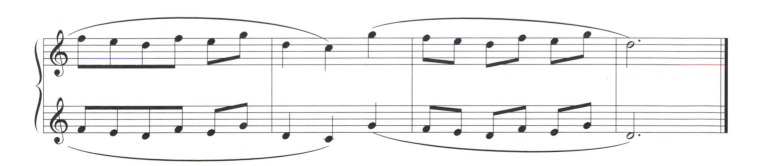

Section Two: Original Works and Arrangements

VANYA
SECONDO

Peter I. Tchaikovsky

AT THE GATE
SECONDO

Peter I. Tchaikovsky

VANYA
PRIMO

Peter I. Tchaikovsky

AT THE GATE
PRIMO

Peter I. Tchaikovsky

Section Two: Original Works and Arrangements

LITTLE PIECE IN G

SECONDO

Anton Bruckner

LITTLE PIECE IN G

PRIMO

Anton Bruckner

Section Two: Original Works and Arrangements

28 I SAW THREE SHIPS

SECONDO

arr. by **David Ferguson**

Barcarolle tempo

Ensemble Music for Group Piano

I SAW THREE SHIPS

PRIMO

arr. by **David Ferguson**

Barcarolle tempo

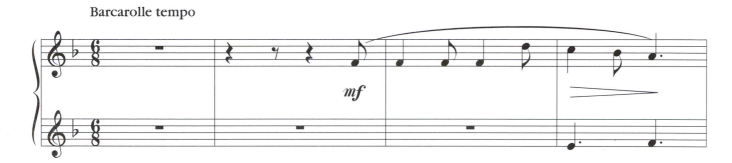

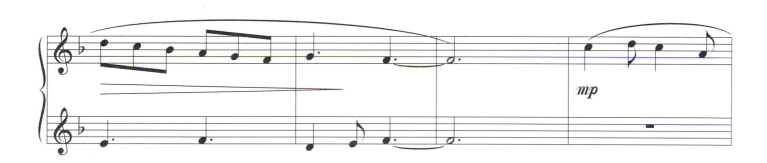

Section Two: Original Works and Arrangements

SECONDO

PRIMO

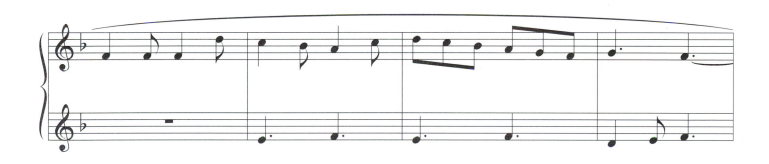

Section Two: Original Works and Arrangements

ROUND DANCE
SECONDO

Bela Bartok
trans. by **Benjamin Suchoff**

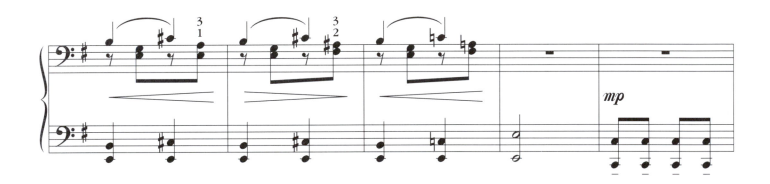

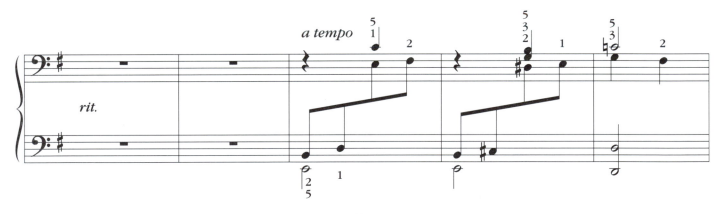

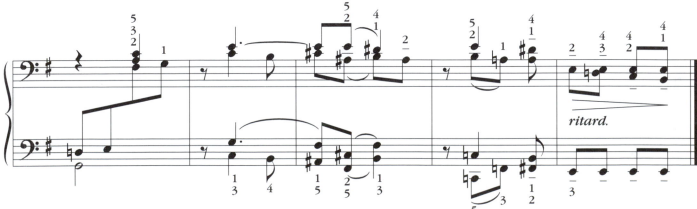

Ensemble Music for Group Piano

ROUND DANCE
PRIMO

Bela Bartok
trans. by **Benjamin Suchoff**

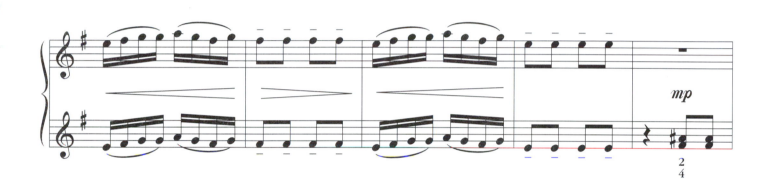

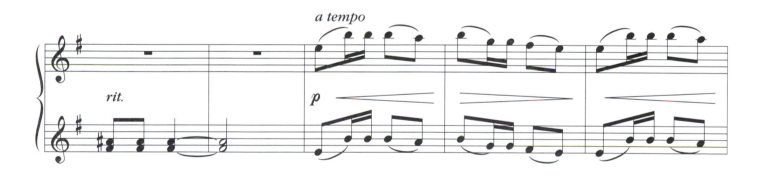

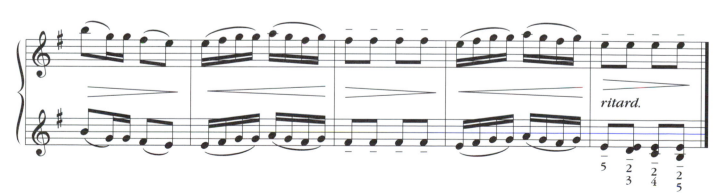

Section Two: Original Works and Arrangements

BALALAIKA
(from *Five Easy Pieces*)

SECONDO

Igor Stravinsky

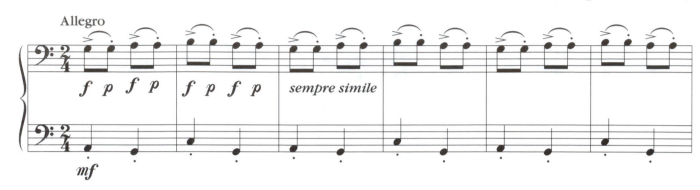

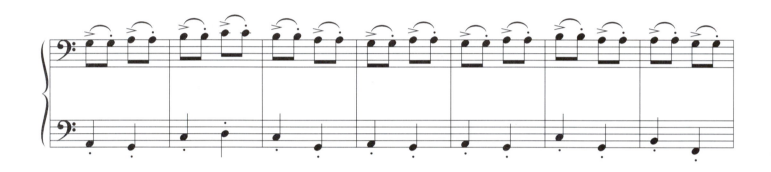

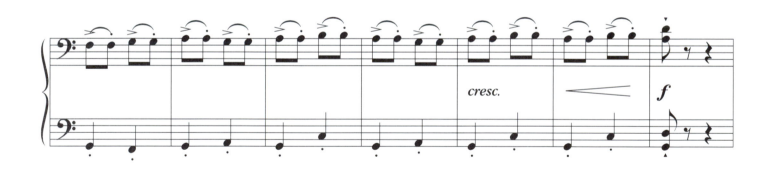

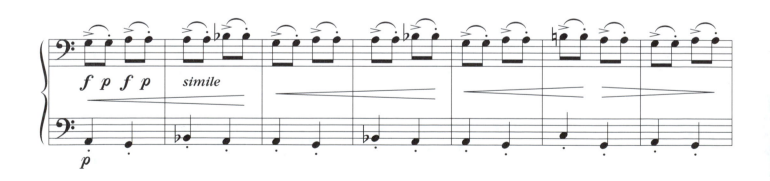

Ensemble Music for Group Piano

BALALAIKA
(from *Five Easy Pieces*)

PRIMO

Igor Stravinsky

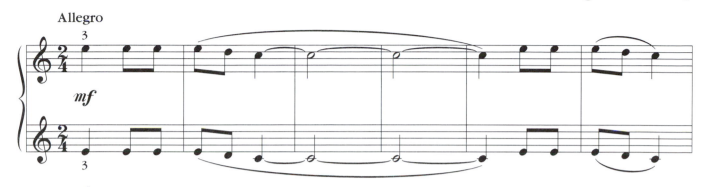

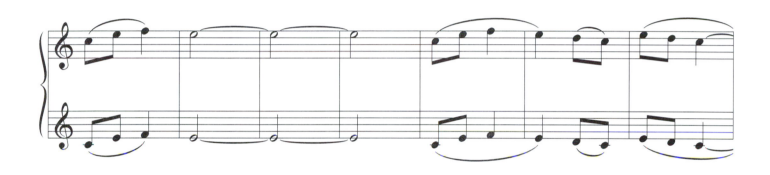

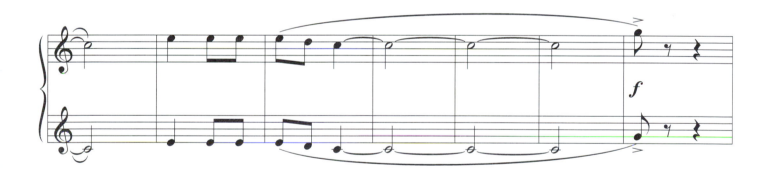

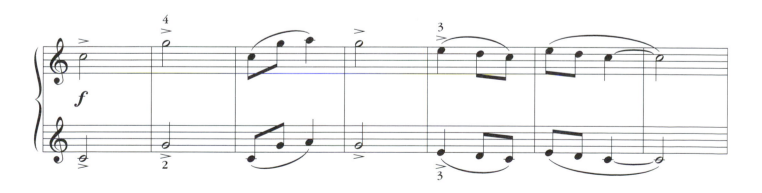

Section Two: Original Works and Arrangements

SECONDO

PRIMO

Section Two: Original Works and Arrangements

SERENADE NO. 8

(Op. 62)

SECONDO

Vincent Persichetti

Ensemble Music for Group Piano

SERENADE NO. 8
(Op. 62)

PRIMO

Vincent Persichetti

Section Two: Original Works and Arrangements

PLAYTIME

SECONDO

Norman Dello Joio

Very lightly (♩. = 72)

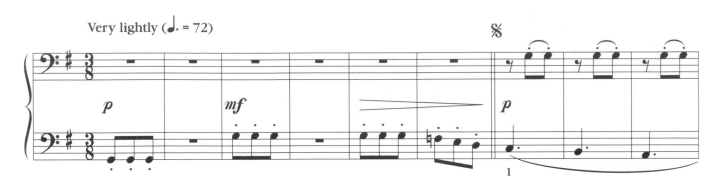

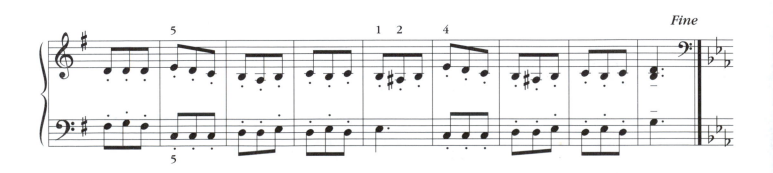

From *Family Album* by Norman Dello Joio by permission of Edward B. Marks Music Corporation.

Ensemble Music for Group Piano

PLAYTIME

PRIMO

Norman Dello Joio

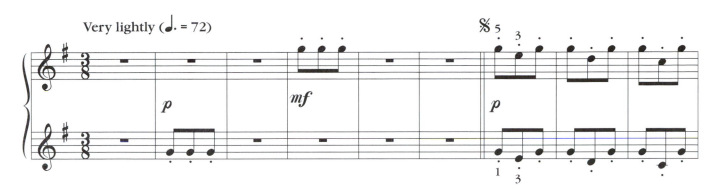

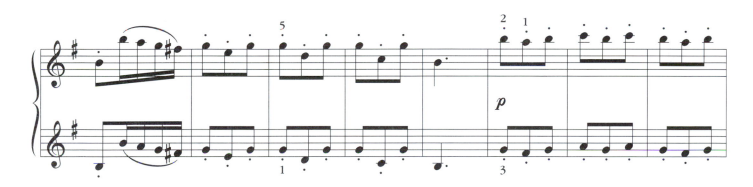

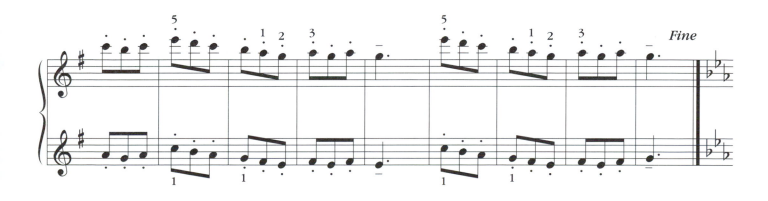

From *Family Album* by Norman Dello Joio by permission of Edward B. Marks Music Corporation.

Section Two: Original Works and Arrangements

SECONDO

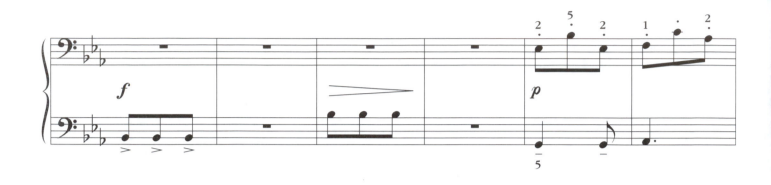

PRIMO

Section Two: Original Works and Arrangements

ALEXANDER'S RAGTIME BAND

SECONDO

music and lyrics by **Irving Berlin**
arr. by **Haydon** and **Lyke**

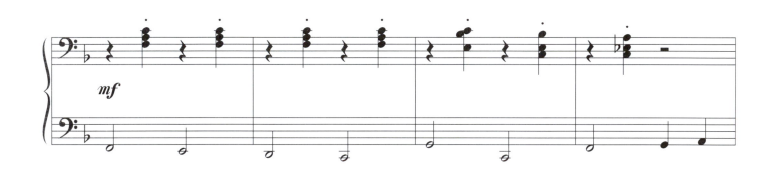

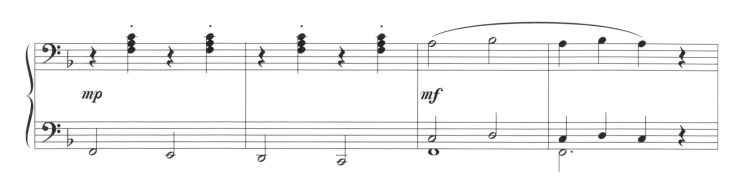

Ensemble Music for Group Piano

ALEXANDER'S RAGTIME BAND

PRIMO

words and music by **Irving Berlin**
arr. by **Haydon** and **Lyke**

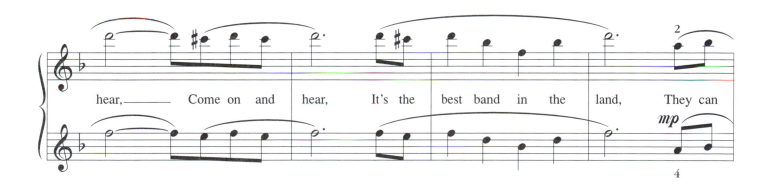

Section Two: Original Works and Arrangements

SECONDO

PRIMO

That's just the best-est band what am, my hon-ey lamb, Come on a-long,____ come on a-long, Let me take you by the hand,____ Up to the man,____ up to the man, who's the lead-er of the band, And if you care to hear the Swan-nee Riv-er played in rag-time,____ Come on and hear,____ Come on and hear Al-ex-an-der's Rag-time Band.

Section Two: Original Works and Arrangements

36 WONDERFUL ONE

SECONDO

music by **Paul Whiteman** and **Ferde Grofe**
words by **Dorothy Terriss**
arr. by **Haydon** and **Lyke**

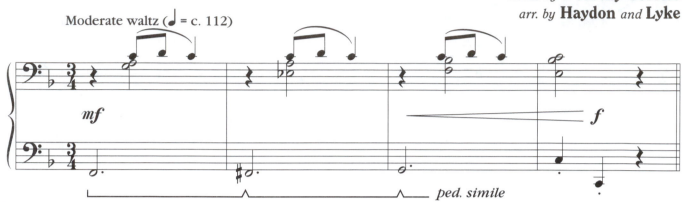

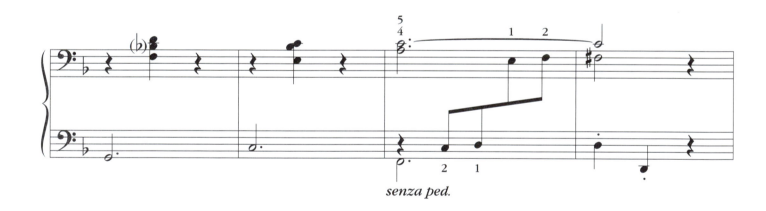

Ensemble Music for Group Piano

WONDERFUL ONE

PRIMO

music by **Paul Whiteman** and **Ferde Grofe**
words by **Dorothy Terriss**
arr. by **Haydon** and **Lyke**

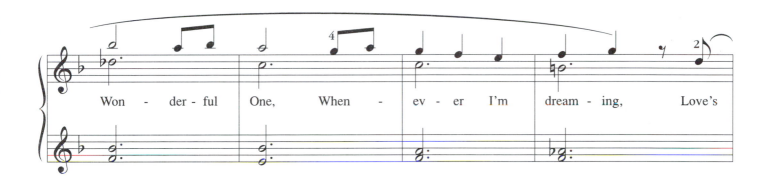

Won - der-ful One, When - ev - er I'm dream - ing, Love's

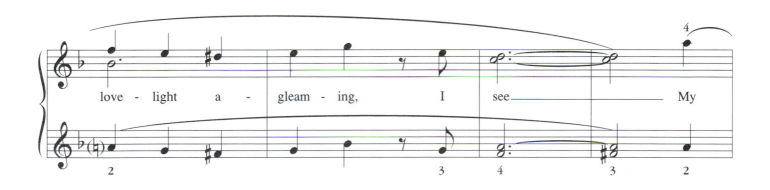

love - light a - gleam - ing, I see ___ My

Won - der-ful One, How my arms ache to hold dear, To

Section Two: Original Works and Arrangements

SECONDO

1

Ensemble Music for Group Piano

PRIMO

Section Two: Original Works and Arrangements

LIMEHOUSE BLUES

SECONDO

words by **Douglas Furber**
music by **Philip Braham**
arr. by **Haydon** and **Lyke**

LIMEHOUSE BLUES

PRIMO

words by **Douglas Furber**
music by **Philip Braham**
arr. by **Haydon** and **Lyke**

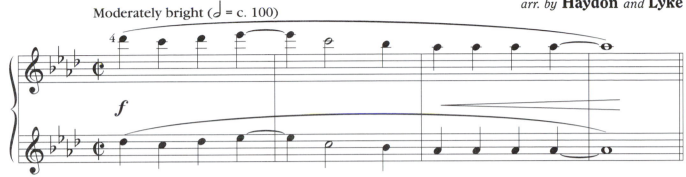

Oh! Lime - house kid,___ Oh! Oh! O! Lime - house kid,___

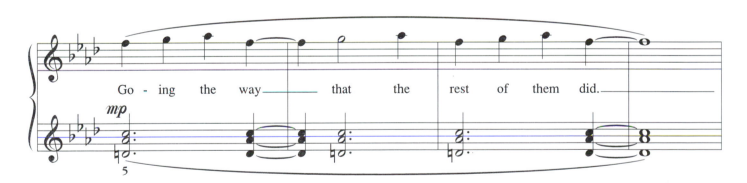

Go - ing the way___ that the rest of them did.

Poor bro - ken blos - som and no - bod - y's child,___

Section Two: Original Works and Arrangements

SECONDO

PRIMO

Section Two: Original Works and Arrangements

SECTION THREE
Arrangements for Multiple Pianos

SARABANDA

Arcangelo Corelli
arr. by **Joan Last**

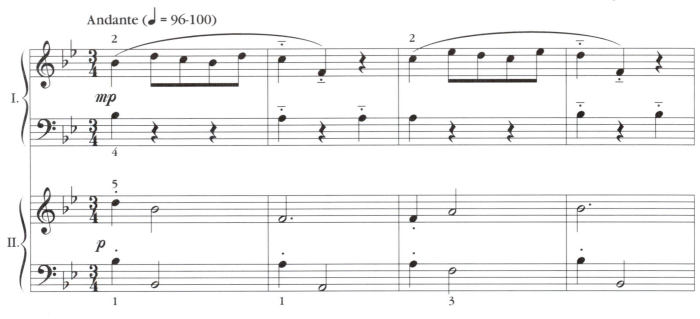

Ensemble Music for Group Piano

 Section Three: Arrangements for Multiple Pianos

MINUET IN G

Johann Sebastian Bach
arr. by **Markham Lee**

From *Four Dance Measures*, by J. S. Bach, arranged by E. Markham Lee.
Copyright 1937 and renewed 1964 by the Oxford University Press. Reprinted by permission

Section Three: Arrangements for Multiple Pianos

86

repeat ad lib.

repeat ad lib.

Ensemble Music for Group Piano

Section Three: Arrangements for Multiple Pianos

40 MINUET

Joseph Haydn
arr. by **George Anson**

Ensemble Music for Group Piano

Section Three: Arrangements for Multiple Pianos

ANDANTE IN E♭

Wolfgang Amadeus Mozart
arr. by **Haydon** *and* **Lyke**

42

WALTZ IN B MINOR

Franz Schubert
arr. by **Haydon** *and* *Lyke*

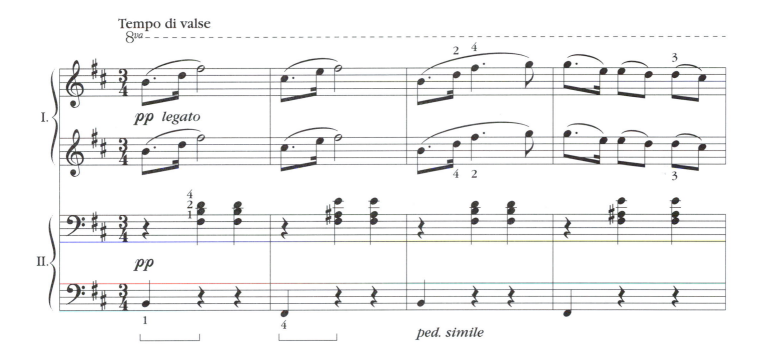

Section Three: Arrangements for Multiple Pianos

Section Three: Arrangements for Multiple Pianos

CANON

Robert Schumann
arr. by **Haydon** *and* **Lyke**

BAMBALINA

music by **Vincent Youmans**
arr. by **Haydon** and **Lyke**

Moderately bright (♩ = 100)

Section Three: Arrangements for Multiple Pianos

Section Three: Arrangements for Multiple Pianos

DAWN

Tony Caramia

Section Three: Arrangements for Multiple Pianos

SLOW MOVEMENT THEME FROM
SYMPHONY NO. 7 *

(Three Pianos or Keyboards)

Ludwig van Beethoven
arr. by **Curtis Smith**

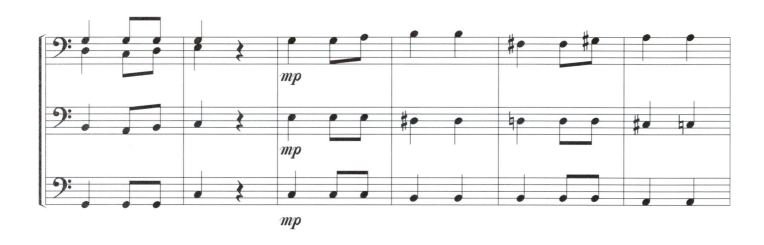

* With this and the following arrangements, create your own orchestrations using the various sampled sounds on your digital piano. Also, determine and mark your own fingerings.

Ensemble Music for Group Piano

Section Three: Arrangements for Multiple Pianos

MAIN THEME, THIRD MOVEMENT
SYMPHONY NO. 3.

(Five Pianos or Keyboards)

Johannes Brahms
arr. by **Curtis Smith**

Un poco allegretto e grazioso

Ensemble Music for Group Piano

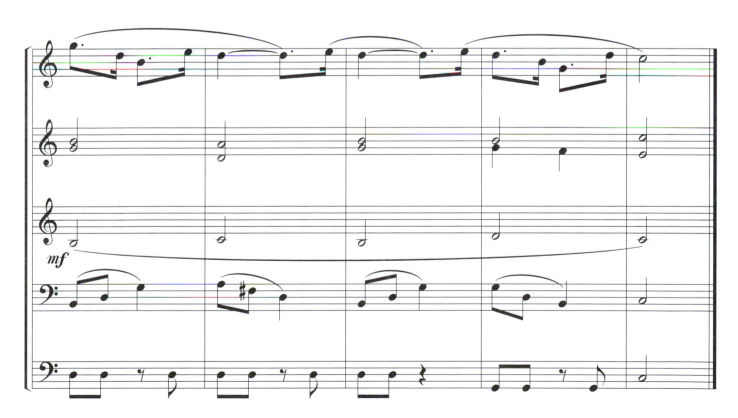

Section Three: Arrangements for Multiple Pianos

LULLABY
(Six Pianos or Keyboards)

Johannes Brahms
arr. by **Bill Keck**

Parts I – IV *8va*

Soft and smooth

Ensemble Music for Group Piano

Section Three: Arrangements for Multiple Pianos

JEANIE WITH THE LIGHT BROWN HAIR

(Six Pianos or Keyboards)

Stephen Foster
arr. by **Bill Keck**

Section Three: Arrangements for Multiple Pianos

THE BAND PLAYED ON
(Six Pianos or Keyboards)

Charles Ward
arr. by **Bill Keck**

Section Three: Arrangements for Multiple Pianos

110

Ensemble Music for Group Piano

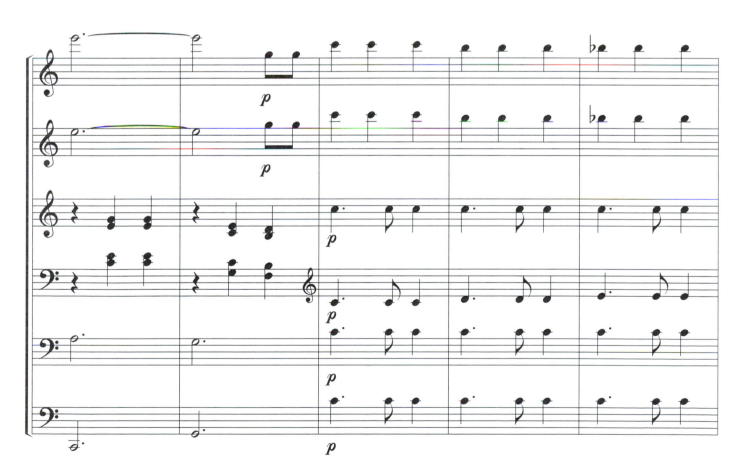

Section Three: Arrangements for Multiple Pianos

Section Three: Arrangements for Multiple Pianos

TRIO FROM
SYMPHONY NO. 7
(Six Pianos or Keyboards)

Franz Schubert
arr. by **Curtis Smith**

Ensemble Music for Group Piano

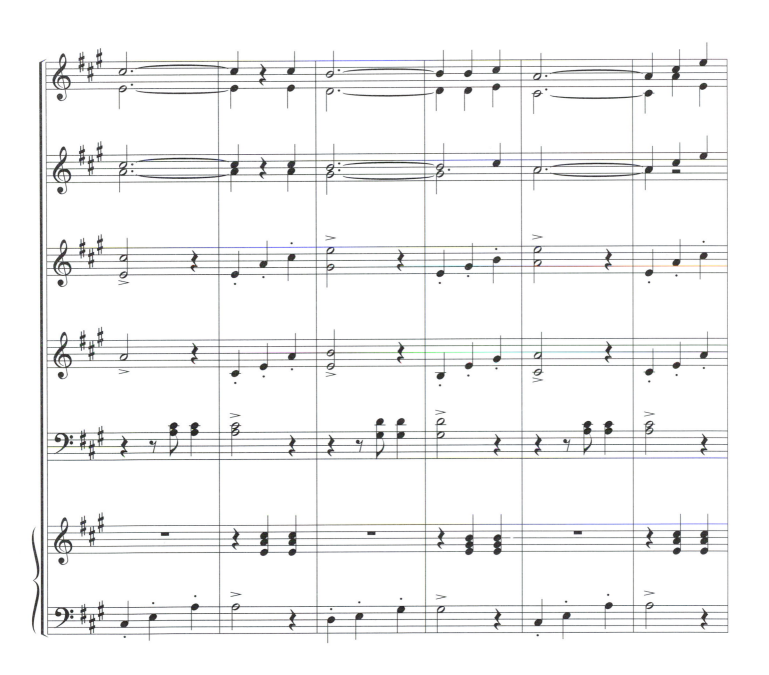

Section Three: Arrangements for Multiple Pianos

Section Three: Arrangements for Multiple Pianos

Ensemble Music for Group Piano

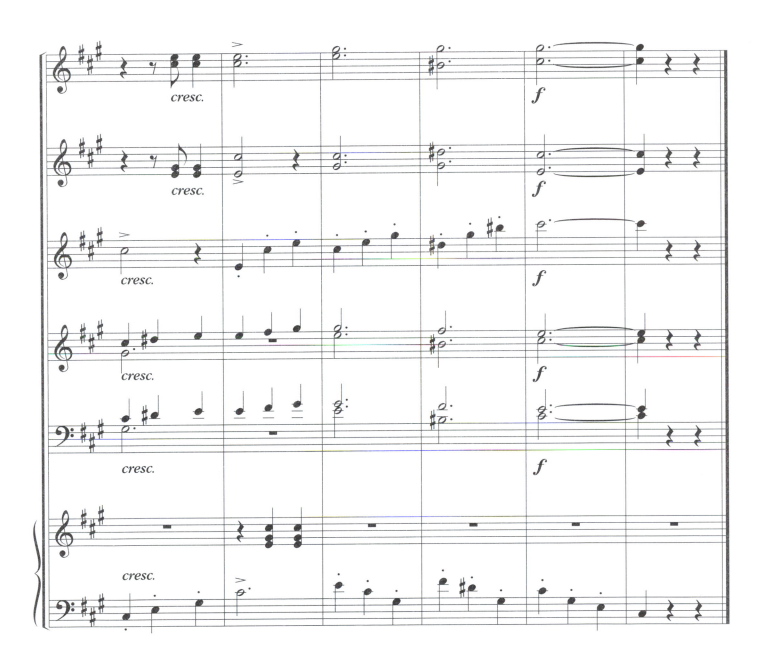

Section Three: Arrangements for Multiple Pianos

C D / M I D I
Accompaniment Tracks

Each track contains a two bar count off; upbeat values are included in the two measures. There are no tracks for music arranged for more than two pianos. (pp. 100–119).

	CD/MIDI Track No.	Title	Page
SECTION ONE Major 5-Finger Primo Patterns (1P4H)	1	Melodious Piece, Op. 149, No. 3	2–5
	2	Melodious Piece, Op. 149, No. 4	6–7
	3	Evening	8–9
	4	Moderato Cantabile (from *First Steps*)	10–13
	5	Melodious Piece, Op. 149, No. 8	14–15
	6	Andante Cantabile, Op. 6, No. 3	16–17
	7	Melodious Piece, Op. 149, No. 9	18–19
	8	On Horseback, Op. 74, No. 2	20–21
	9	Hunting, Op. 81, No. 3	22–23
SECTION ONE Minor 5-Finger Primo Patterns (1P4H)	10	Funeral For A Bird, Op. 74, No. 1	24–25
	11	Allegretto in C Minor	26–27
	12	Mama Scolds, Op. 74, No. 4	28–29
	13	Romance in A Minor, Op. 6, No. 1	30–31
	14	Romance in G Minor, Op. 149, No. 11	32–33
	15	Gray Day, Op. 74, No. 3	34–35
SECTION TWO Original Works and Arrangements (1P4H)	16, 17	German Dance in C	36–37
	18	German Dance in B♭	38–39
	19	Dance, Op. 824, No. 18	40–41
	20	Allegro Non Troppo	42–45
	21, 22	Lændler	46–47
	23	My Braids	48–49
	24	There Was No Wind	48–49
	25	Vanya	50–51
	26	At The Gate	50–51
	27	Little Piece in G	52–53
	28	I Saw Three Ships	54–57
	29	Round Dance	58–59
	30	Balalaika (from *Five Easy Pieces*)	60–63
	31, 32	Serenade No. 8, Op. 62	64–65
	33, 34	Playtime	66–69
	35	Alexander's Ragtime Band	70–73
	36	Wonderful One	74–77
	37	Limehouse Blues	78–81
SECTION THREE Arrangements for Multiple Pianos	38	Sarabanda	82–84
	39	Minuet in G	85–87
	40	Minuet	88–89
	41	Andante in E♭	90
	42	Waltz in B Minor	91–93
	43	Canon	94
	44	Bambalina	95–97
	45	Dawn	98–99

Ensemble Music for Group Piano